# SOBRIETY
# AND
# STRENGTH

# FIRST AND MOST IMPORTANTLY

I feel it is important to talk about why I wrote this book. I've written "Alcoholism And Its Stories" which talks about the destructive nature associated with alcoholism, as well as a little bit of help in regards to sobriety. I also wrote "A Book

Of Alcoholism Vol. 1&2" which talks about all things in regards to alcoholism. Yet I feel those books are merely stepping stones to something bigger. A goal of mine is to help people, people who may be confused, or who can not relate to the problems they are facing. For me, when I was struggling, internet searches, and literature was not something that really helped me. So years later, I am writing what I wished I had had when I needed help. Maybe someone will relate to this, maybe some won't. However, you might learn something in this book!

I will talking about my life, and vaguely talking about others I have met in my journey of sobriety, as well as things I have learned along the way! Unfortunately too many people die from alcohol related causes, and I was someone who almost became part of that statistic. Luckily I was able to pull through and improve upon myself. Let me see if my story can help you as well!

*This is Sobriety And Strength, and it is dedicated to those who are suffering from alcohol problems, as well as those whose lives, and families have been destroyed by alcoholism. Thank you. Stay strong!*

# CONTENTS

# I LOOKED BACK AT MYSELF IN DISGUST

March, 13th, 2017.

A cold morning, with brisk winds blowing through the trees. The sky as overcast as my mood. Walking outside at 4 am onto my balcony, I look down on the street to see emptiness. In a rather unusual way, I always preferred these hours, however I also despised them. A night owl at heart, I found the middle of the night to be rather lonely. A good part of the world is asleep.

I remember a mirror I had in my living room. Towards the end of my stint with alcohol abuse, I refused to look at myself in it. Mostly due to the fact, that once ago I was a rather skinny guy, who usually dressed nice, and was rather clean cut, but unfortunately lost my way. To which then I had become very much overweight, bloated, and pale. I dressed more so casual as well… well casual is one way to put it. Which is ironically something that I still do to this day, mostly because of comfort. I truly despised myself, and my appearance. On this day (March 13th) I decided to take a look.

*"I see a guy in his early twenties looking back at me, almost like a cry for help, yet at the same time a need to keep being destructive to himself. Overweight, pale, and very much so unhealthy. Miserable eyes, and little to no life left left in them. It was me, and I had lost myself" -Self Observation*

On this day, I nearly lost my life. It was the day I got help. It was the day that broke me, and it was the day in which my life changed forever. For better, and for

worse. Why worse? Because I would have
to face sobriety.

   Having a somewhat medical
background in pharmacy, and spending so
much more time studying other subjects
to learn more. (I was extremely ambitious,
and I wanted to know as much as possible,
so I could be more than what I was when I
decided to work, or go back to school.) I
knew what would happen if I went to the
hospital, and everything I thought would
happen, ended up happening. But it was
worse than I imagined.

   I anticipated being put in intensive
care, and being sedated, as well as out of
my mind. What I wasn't aware of though,

was the psychological damage I would get from that experience. It destroyed me. Over the span of this book I will write more about some of the experiences. But I wanted to give a glimpse into my life.

The way I felt on that day cannot really be described. The only words I can use are **devastation**, and **hatred**. Devastation, because of how mentally unstable I was for so long leading up to that day, and hatred, because of how much I hated myself for what I put myself through.

Are you for example in a state where you are mentally unstable? Maybe perhaps you are making all the wrong choices, and furthering yourself down a hole? Maybe you are like me, where you become so oblivious to what you are doing, and you think you are happy, and content, but really just on autopilot and slowly losing grip on your own reality! I was a ticking time bomb. Anger didn't help either, because with anger, you might become irrational, and when you are irrational, the decisions you make are affected by that.

Just know that I don't have all the answers, but perhaps I can use myself to maybe give you some perspective, and more awareness into your own life. With more awareness, you might be more encouraged to fix your own problems.

*"You can't find a solution to a problem, if you don't know that there is a problem"*
*-Important Info*

What had I become? The very shell of the person I was before. The person I was before, wasn't happy, but I was in a better mental state than on the day of March 13th, 2017. Alcohol destroyed me. It destroyed my mental health, it nearly killed me, the withdrawals from it were terrible, and it affected my decision making in nearly every single way. I would use alcohol for multiple reasons, such as depression, or maybe I felt as if my mind was running 100 miles per hour, and it slowed it down for me. The list goes on.

Point being, is that I used it far too much, and for the wrong reasons. What started out as pleasure, ended with pain. That is the lovely(sarcasm) part of addiction.

It was time for a change, and I almost didn't make the change. To this day, even with relapses, and significant cravings at times, I am glad I did. Because it gave me a chance to live! I sincerely wish I could drink to this very day, but I know I can't. I can't put myself back in that position, because I might not make it through next time if it were to happen again.

Is it time for a change reader?

# YOU CAME TO HELP, I CAME WITH ANGER

When I was engulfed in addiction, I was irrational. Let me explain. I was starting my shift, and was sober. I was dealing with withdrawals however. I was extremely shaky, my heart was racing, my anxiety was bad, and I was not wanting to be at work. So 10 minutes into starting my shift, I walk out of my work, and drive away. While getting onto the freeway, I hit a curb that I always seemed to hit no matter what, and my tire blew. Instead of pulling over onto the shoulder, I proceeded to drive a mile on a blown tire to a gas station. After I got there, I realized I had no way of changing my tire, I called my father for help. While he was on his way, I go inside the gas station and buy three pint size bottles of vodka and just for reference, **1 Pint is 375 ml, and a standard wine bottle is usually 750 ml**.

After the purchase, and while my father was on the way, I decided to drink 1 full pint, and another half pint of vodka in the bathroom. I started to feel relief finally. My father shows up not too soon after that, and notices I am under the influence, and tries to help me figure out my tire, as well as giving me a field sobriety test (he is a former police detective) to which I failed with flying colors. He noticed there was obviously a problem, and he asks for the bottles I bought, and any in my car as well. Keep in mind, this isn't the first time he has seen me act like this. I hand him all the bottles, except for one, which I was hiding in my jacket.(He was giving me a ride home, and I had no way of getting to a gas station once I got home...)

He was obviously worried for me, and I wasn't really caring that much at the time. I was also pissed at him as well. Though I didn't show my anger towards him until later. I was playing everything down, and he was just listening on the way home. It was a mundane car ride really. My mother however? She definitely didn't hide her anger towards me. She let me have it. And as usual I didn't care to hear it.

There were other moments like this. I was an absolute mess, and other people were paying for it too. It was a gradual loss of control. I had problems for years, but it wasn't until the last 6 months before getting help, that I was getting sloppy. This is a common thing I have seen with other people. At some point, it starts to overtake you.

Now let's talks about how badly I messed up in this situation.

1. My grandfather had died not too long before this event happened. My

grandfather died of alcohol related causes. I was drunk when my father told me. So this didn't help him.

2. I walked out on my job.

3. I got intoxicated in a gas station bathroom while my father was on the way to help me. What was I thinking?

4. I didn't fully grasp how much people were putting up with.

5. My own father had to give me a field sobriety test. Imagine that.

6. I shouldn't have driven so long on a blown tire at freeway speeds. It did damage.

This wasn't the first, or last time I've put the burden on my parents before. You see, they often tried to help, but I responded with anger. It was ungrateful, and poor behavior on my part! I look back with disgust at how I treated them, and for what I put them through. One of the big reasons that I was so angry with them, was the fact that I worried they would do some sort of intervention, or even force me to get help. I didn't want to quit using alcohol, and I felt as if they were a threat to that. So naturally, I got defensive, and then proceeded to shut them out of my life. Only on some occasions would I speak to them.

The events with the blown tire occurred in November, 2016. Let's talk about the next month, December. I remember my father randomly showed up at my apartment. Mostly due to the fact that I had not responded for a while. He was worried I was dead. His father was found dead in November. I invited him in, hesitantly, and my apartment had empty bottles everywhere. I remember telling him that I threw a party, and he responded with something that bothered me to no end. He said *"This reminds me of how my dads house was when I was younger."*

If there is one thing that bothers me, is when I get compared to someone else. I wasn't my grandfather, and I didn't even know him. Throw in some denial of my own problems, and I was angry! It only made my motivation to stop talking to loved ones stronger. I just wasn't ready to get help. I got sloppy and it was more obvious to others of my problem. I never threw a party either. That was a lie to justify the amount of bottles in the apartment. Normally I was better at hiding it, such as in 2013, I had a large drawer that had about 15 empty bottles of vodka in it. Living with my mother at the time, she didn't know. There was a time about a year later, where she found bottles in another drawer of mine. I assume she just thought it was just me being a young adult who's having too much fun. No big deal.

Anyways, i got sloppy over time, as I was losing control of my own self. Which can happen.

Assuming you are wondering whether or not you are an alcoholic, or maybe seeking help, i want to end this chapter with this. I find it to be rather sobering being on both sides, both as an alcoholic, who is responding with anger, and also on the receiving end of anger from an alcoholic. Do you get defensive over the things I got defensive over? Do you feel as if you are taking things out on people who are trying to help? I get it, sometimes I get annoyed at people who try to help me, but in regards to substance, maybe think about whether or not your defensiveness could be a sign of a problem. Basically, if someone is concerned about your drinking, think about it for a second. If someone is worried about you like that, maybe you should take the time to listen. It's almost unsettling how oblivious we can be, yet our actions are so obvious to another person.

# SOME THINGS FROM MY HOSPITAL VISIT

I'll take a moment to talk about just how miserable my hospital visit was. As well as what I went through. I feel as if I did not describe it as well in my previous works. The reason why I do this to give you examples of how you might be able to relate to me, or maybe not. Maybe you can't relate, but you can understand/listen. Plus people in meetings/rehab were often interested, as we listen to how others got

to where they were. so you might be too!
Let's now talk about the ultra fun(sarcasm)
things I went through.

**1. I was confused beyond anything I'd
ever experienced before.**

And it was different than being
confused as to where your car is, or
waking up after getting an hour of sleep,
and you are confused a little. This kind of
confusion was different. Imagine for
example, that you think you are a pilot,
and you actually believe you are a pilot
when you are really not! That's the
confusion I was experiencing, but in a
much more crazy way. I had a ultra vivid

dream on day 2 in the ICU, where I was at my elementary school with all my teachers. We were having a mattress race down the long driveway to the school. Imagine that? I remember my mattress was gliding down concrete so fast! When I awoke from this dream, I was determined to go to the mattress race in real life! Problem was, was that I was an ICU patient with severe alcohol withdrawals, wanting to escape the hospital to go to see my old teachers and ride mattresses...

To make it worse, I believed it to be true for quite a bit. I didn't know why I couldn't go to the mattress race, and I didn't know who these people were, or who I was for that matter! And what the hell are all these tubes connected to my body?! And woah! When did THIS tube get in there...?! I'm referring to a catheter. Luckily I was sedated beforehand.

## 2. To this day I don't know if this happened!

At some during my stay in the ICU, i had "behavioral issues" and was restrained to my bed. It was terrifying. Due to my confusion, imagine not knowing who you are, or where you are, but you are restrained? It's a freaky feeling. And I have wondered for years as to why I was restrained.

The number one thing I can think of, may not even be true. What I remember is this... I was in a stairwell in my hospital gown, surrounded by about 8 different medical professionals, who were telling me that it will be okay, and I panic and start trying to run! As I tried to run, I fell over, and then it was lights out for me.

There is a problem with this story though. I don't know if it was true. Was it reality? A dream? I was hallucinating quite a bit in the hospital as well. What could be the case? Well, to this day, I still don't know. I could have been restrained for any reason. Perhaps I was pulling out my IV lines. Though, if that was the case, why would my legs also be restrained? It bothers me, because I don't know what happened. There wasn't some friend who was like "Oh man do you remember last night? We have it on video" to tell me.

### 3. I was traumatized to end.

The hospital staff treated me very well honestly. I wasn't traumatized by them, I was traumatized by my situation. For the moments that I was "there" in the head, I was scared to death. I genuinely felt like I was going to die, because of how the situation felt for me. When I would briefly snap out of my confusion, I was scared that I was experiencing it(confusion). And I kept hearing screams in my ears, and random voices saying "come here". And I thought at first that the screams were because I was in a hospital. I mean screams aren't that uncommon there. And also that maybe the staff was saying "come here" to me. However, neither one was the case.

I would also see things that weren't there. Such as a throne with a clown on it at the end of my bed, to which I begged the clown to get my restraints off. It's true, and it didn't work. I would see people that weren't actually there. Not hospital staff, but just random people, as well as moving shadows that were chasing each other across the room. Even more unusual? At least to me, was my mother's voice calling my name directly into my ear. She hadn't arrived at the hospital, due to her being out of state! It's one thing to hear random voices, but when I heard a familiar voice, it was even scarier. It felt as if anytime I would wake up, I would get put right back under again. That was scary too. I had always been afraid of getting surgery due to anesthesia, so the thought of being put down, and not waking up, scared the hell out of me. Yet here I was, on repeat it seemed. It made time go by quick though! But in all seriousness though, I didn't know what was going on most of the time, so if I had died due to my withdrawals in that time, I would have died not knowing who I was, or where I was at most likely.

People have died due to alcohol withdrawals. I'm shocked some people don't know that. But yes, people can die from it. I could have died from it. My body was freaking out. My kidneys were failing, my potassium levels were far too low. Stuff was going on with my liver as well. All in my early twenties. My memory is blurry from that time in the hospital, but I did my best explaining this to you. As crazy as some things sounded, they all appeared real to me. Can you imagine that? Let me introduce you to "Destruction By Alcoholism".

# LETTING GO OF ALCOHOLISM
# AND ITS STORIES

What do you do when you are an author, and your book is doing surprisingly good, and you just can't even bother with it? That's the case with a previous book. It's called "Alcoholism And Its Stories". It's doing good at the time of writing this, especially in the U.K, which is rather shocking. It was my real first attempt at writing a book. However, I made errors, and I can't get myself to want to go and revise it. You see, I am going to keep pushing the book, and let it continue to sell on the market. It has a good story in it called "Destruction By Alcoholism". That is the only reason why it is still out there. However, what I am going to do is take some things from it, and put it into this book. Don't worry I am getting to the self help part momentarily. I just wanted to point this out. Flaws may have come out of that book, but I wouldn't be here without it! And since this book, besides another one of mine called "Three Sides In One", is my attempt at changing everything, I will give it my best. By the way, you may have already noticed that my writing style is more personal, and almost as if I am talking to you in conversation, versus just writing everything out, and leaving it at that!

So along with with Volume 2 of "A Book Of Alcoholism", I will be including "Destruction By Alcoholism" because of how important it is to me, and my writing career!

# DESTRUCTION BY ALCOHOLISM

# 1. JASON

L"Desperation is the very thing that can destroy a person. Especially when it comes to substance. How do you know if you have a problem with substance? Or if someone you love has a problem with substance?

There are hundreds of articles that will tell you the signs of struggle, but it isn't so clear cut. There is a lot more to it. Alcohol, for example, is a major substance! A substance that, for a lot of people, can be used responsibly, but for others? It can destroy families, lives, careers, and so on.

Addiction knows no boundaries, rich or poor, male or female, different races etc. If there was an easy fix to this, or if money could fix this, then people wouldn't be destroying their own lives, and people wouldn't be dying."

Jason, a 27 year old male who did a lot of different jobs, suffered from alcoholism for the past 9 years. He lost his job mostly because he could not leave the house sober. Jasons withdrawals were very bad, and instead of getting help, he kept drinking, and dug himself into a deeper hole.

A guy in his twenties, he never thought this would have happened. He never thought that he would get to a point where his body would freak out without alcohol. Losing relationships, and cutting ties with his family members, he became more isolated, more alone, more at a loss for words as to what he had done with his life.

40 shots of vodka every day, throughout the day to control the withdrawals. Draining his bank account, and losing control further and further until he lost his own mind. Jasons story as you are reading this, sounds all over the place doesn't it? That's because his mind was all over the place. Alcoholism can destroy, so this is not a story of happiness, or hope, but a story to try to give people a better idea as to why it is such a serious matter. There wont be any dialogue in this story either. It was written and told from my perspective. Maybe this hits close to home for you, maybe it doesn't.

So... lets move further. Jason was pretty kind hearted, however he made mistakes, and had a great family and home life. And like i said, alcoholism has no boundaries or restrictions. Jason was very much loved by his mother and father, and his siblings. He didn't do so good in school however, as his mind was in other places.

He had underlying issues, such as depression and anxiety. And he was put on medications at the age of 14 at the urging of his medical team. The anxiety was mostly described as irrational, and sometimes erratic. Sometimes there wasn't a cause, just about anything could give him anxiety. Depression on the other hand could not be explained. And Its frustrating that for some people, the cause of their depression is known, for instance the loss of a family member, or Post-Partum Depression. But what if your cause just isn't known? What if it is just there? Some say chemical imbalance, who knows.

Regardless, treatment via medications started at 14, and from there on he would would go through puberty to adulthood with struggles. Jason had hopes and dreams like any other person, however, as most people know, as we get older our goals and realities are changed based on what happens around us. Jason, for instance wanted to be an oncologist, which is a doctor that specializes in cancer. A difficult job, to say the least, but Jason? Well he had the personality and ability to deal with things like that.

However, in school he did not do so well, and later on, substance took over his life and things changed!

Jason also wanted to be a writer, but that also complicated things as his creativity dwindled away into nothing in his early twenties. So job wise, Jason did many things, such as fast food, delivery driver work, and he made music. It wasn't what he wanted, but it was all he could really do.

In this story i will be talking about the second week of March, 2017. Jason, at 27 years old dies in the early morning hours of march 14th, 2017. This story is to talk about the week leading up to that.

# 2. MARCH 7TH

Jason was on day 4 of being awake without getting any sleep. This really hit him hard to say the least! By day 3, he was having auditory hallucinations, starting out as hearing random faint voices. Alcohol wasn't helping him sleep anymore, and neither were his medications. He just could not sleep by any means.

On day 3, things progressed rather drastically! Imagine your are just sitting there on your couch, and you can hear your name being called, and its not just like a voice coming from another room. But a voice you can just hear from inside your head. Throughout the day, he ignored calls and messages form different people as he was in his own head freaking out.

Two shots of vodka every hour, sometimes three depending on how his withdrawals were at that given time. He was trying to watch tv, relax, and trying to yet again sleep. The voices were getting louder, the alcohol numbed him enough to not be too panicked over it however. That wasn't going to help for much longer though!

Louder, and more frequent was his name being called as we get to day 4, March 7th. Jason starts to hear screams, and unfortunately sleep deprivation is known to cause hallucinations of different kinds.

Jason just needed sleep, but he could not sleep because of the screams. It was devastating, almost as if he was **mentally being destroyed by a baseball bat**. Now Its about 2 am on March 7th, and Jason puts on headphones, and then proceeds to put on a random show. Blasting the volume, he can still hear the screams, but they're being muffled to a point.

Panicking, and eventually getting up and pacing, he didn't know what to do. Losing his mind further, Jason desperately needed sleep but couldn't. So thats when Jason downed 8 shots of vodka, and decided to take twice the amount of sleep medication he had if he needed it.

He had already taken it earlier, but it just didn't work, and hadn't been working! So he made a reckless decision to take more than prescribed, and in combination of alcohol, which wasn't safe. And Jason, with headphones blasting, and the room spinning, vomits, and then proceeds to lay down on the cold bathroom floor. He finally is able to get some sleep!

He slept on the bathroom floor for 6 hours or so before his body starts jerking around beyond anything a normal mind could fathom. Dazed and out of his mind, he goes to get more to drink. Hands shaking like crazy, and a neck, and body jerking around , he proceeds to drink about 3 shots to start the day.

Sitting on the couch, in shock about the night previous, he is glad to not hear voices anymore.

But Jason is now in a major state of depression, a depression beyond anything he had ever felt before. He wasn't suicidal, but he knew health wise, he was going downhill. He wouldn't take his own life, yet he didn't want to do anything about saving it either. And it was becoming more apparent to him that he  was growing weaker, and weaker by the day.

Going up or down a staircase was almost impossible. His ability to walk was decreasing, and his heart rate was consistently in the 130 BPM range no matter what he was doing. As time went on  Jasons body starts to calm down as the alcohol was kicking in, though in about an hour or two his withdrawals would kick in again.

March 7th, was significant for two reasons. One, because of how the absolute destruction sleep deprivation can have on someone already in a seriously bad mental state. And two, the thoughts Jason was having in regards to his alcohol problems, he didn't want help, instead he opted to do nothing. Which would mean that he would eventually die from what he was doing.

"I feel as if I'm lost in a foggy forest at night. You can't see ahead of you, you are all alone, and what you can see is unknown to you." - A Sick Mind

Jason isn't any different than others who have struggled with alcohol problems. Everyone has a story, some worse, some better than others. Regardless everyone has one. This one so far at least, has its fair share of crazy to it.

Jason didn't suffer from withdrawals though. It was a gradual thing. The drinking became a bit more excessive and withdrawal symptoms started to occur, and

Jason, hoping to ease the withdrawals, would drink more and thus a pattern would start. And as time went on, Jasons body became so used to it, and things gradually got worse. The hole kept getting deeper and, like a lot of alcoholics, they often feel hopeless in that hole! If you didn't already know too much about alcoholics, is that they are all different people, with somewhat similar problems. No person is the same, and that can be said of many, if not all alcoholics. The stories, the cravings, how it all started, often times are similar, but not always similar with alcoholics.

Reader, if there is one thing i want you to get from this story, it is this. **Most of us never meant to be here on purpose.**

# 3. MARCH 8TH

The apartment is an absolute wreck, however Jason physically cannot clean it. It is essentially destroyed. Bottles everywhere, trash everywhere, weird smells, and the shell of a person living within it all.

Jason, on this day, woke up in a panic, and considered asking for help. Considering the possibility he could be fixed, however, upon putting the number of his father on the phone, he stops. He doesn't see a point. **He doesn't feel like he can live without alcohol, at least not**

**happily**. From Jasons perspective, his surroundings were destroyed, he himself felt destroyed, and he didn't exactly treat his mother or father kindly for quite a while. They were patient with him, but Jason kept digging his hole deeper and would lie.

Since Jason lived alone, he didn't have anyone around him, which meant he got to live his life how he wanted too, which was a good, and bad thing. It was good because Jason had his freedom, but bad because had he not been alone, maybe someone would have kept him in check.

Later into the day Jason needed more alcohol, so he decided to walk to a nearby gas station. He could tell the people around him knew he had a problem. The looks he would get were often looks of pity. Jason would buy bottle of vodka, and whilst shaking, would swipe his card. No one ever said anything to him, instead they would just give him a smile and sometimes would ask how he is doing.

**What was once a guy who typically was clean shaven and dressed nice, was now a guy with unkept facial hair, who became overweight, very pale, shaky, and weak.** Jason proceeded to walk home and would dread going up the stairs to his apartment. Walking inside, Jason immediately starts to cry, and drops his bag of alcohol on the carpet. Not because of the looks he got from people, but from what he didn't have. Walks, and sometimes showers were often the times where Jason would do his deepest thinking.

Jason wanted someone to save him, however he cut everyone out of his life, excluding some family members who instead just left him alone. What do you do if you want love, but your own life is so messed up at the moment, that it wouldn't be fair to that person. And on top of that, not having the will to fix yourself either.

Not too long after all of this occurred Jason started to see someone in his apartment. It was his mother, but it wasn't. He closed his eyes for a second and then reopened only to find it was just in his head. Things were significantly going downhill for him, and this was really put in his head when he looked in the mirror and just saw what looked back at him.

Reader, i am constantly bringing up his appearance, and how he sees himself for a reason. The reason why is because it is astounding how substance can absolutely affect how ones appearance can be. It is like those pictures of people before and after meth. It is also important to note that Jason wasn't the type to think his problems were worse than others. For himself it was the worst, but he knew all to well that there were people out there who were suffering from severe illness of all different kinds.

If you think you are having a bad day, just remember that right there is a kid who is most likely dying from cancer, and wishing they had more time.

This final week i am writing about is filled with significant and insignificant things. This isn't supposed to be a long story, but a kind of short, and detailed point i am trying to make. Just like the short life of Jason. There could have been more, but there isn't. Get it?

# 4. MARCH 9TH THROUGH 12TH

*"A journal is a significant thing. It not only is a time capsule, but also a therapist in book. Looking back on it can provide insight into ones past, and also is a reminder of where one was"*

Jasons got out his journal and wrote as follows...

"March 9th 2017. I AM FED UP AND I CAN NOT DO THIS ANYMORE! I HAVE LOST EVERYTHING, I AM LOSING MYSELF, I HAVE DESTROYED EVERY SINGLE THING I HAVE HELD DEAR, AND FOR WHAT?! FOR FUCKING WHAT! THIS IS NOT FAIR! HOW IS IT THAT SOMEONE IN THEIR TWENTIES CAN HAVE A FUCKING ALCOHOL PROBLEM! WHO DID I PISS OFF? I CANT GO TO A GROCERY STORE WITHOUT HAVING SOMEONE LOOK AT ME LIKE I AM INSANE! I CANT HELP THE SHAKING! I AM SO SICK OF DOING THE WALK OF SHAME AT 7 IN THE MORNING TO GET MORE ALCOHOL WHILE OTHERS ARE

GOING TO GET COFFEE AND GO TO
WORK! I CANT GO UP OR DOWN A
STAIRCASE WITHOUT MY LEGS
TREMBLING TO THE POINT THAT I
MAY FALL. I HAVE LOST LOVE
BECAUSE ID RATHER DRINK, I
FUCKING CANT STAND MY FAMILY. I
KNOW THEY ARE TRYING TO HELP
AND I KNOW THEY KNOW I HAVE
PROBLEM BUT I DONT GIVE A SHIT
WHAT THEY THINK AND THEY CAN
GO FUCK THEMSELVES IF THEY
THINK I WOULD ACCEPT HELP IF
THEY OFFERED. I WONT BE OFFING
MY SELF BUT ILL PROBABLY BE
FOUND DEAD BEFORE TOO LONG
AND I DONT HONESTLY CARE IF

THATS THE CASE. I AM MISERABLE AND I CANNOT IMAGINE A LIFE WITHOUT ALCOHOL. MEDICATION HAS NOT DONE ANYTHING FOR ME, THERAPY HAS NOT DONE ANYTHING FOR EITHER. I AM HELPLESS AND I AM OKAY WITH IT! END OF STORY! FUCK. YOU. ALL!"

This was all of out of place for Jason to write as he loved his family for instance. However in his sick mind, he felt so much conflict, and so much confusion that he went on a rant. With the feeling of nothing helping his life, nor wanting any help of any sort he wrote what he felt, while at the same time wishing someone would help him.

This is a good example of how substance can warp someone's mind, turning them into a completely different person. Jason was still in there, but he was losing grip of his own reality. Combining the 4 days of no sleep, with hearing screams, and his name being yelled through his own head. To realizing his former self being was shattered to a million pieces, it was a recipe for mental health disaster. What could he possibly do?

# 5. MARCH 12TH

Things had steadily stayed the same for Jason since writing that entry. Nothing significant happened in the meantime. However, things went downwards on the 12th and final day before seeking help. Here's what led him here, and this is a problem a lot of people have unfortunately. It's when a problem becomes so big and you don't ask for help and you try to fix it yourself.

Reader? How often have you been able to fix a problem that has become so big? Before i move further towards the end of this, i need to give background. So lets recap. Jason has struggled for years with alcohol problems, he has lost love, friendship, family relationships have shattered, his job, his ambitions, and his will to want to live. If you talk to any alcoholic i would assume they would say one of those things happened to them. Sometimes people get the help they need early on, and have the ability to fix their lives, some it becomes too late and they feel they can't fix anything. This is Jasons case.

**Do you know a Jason in your life?**

Continuing on, Jason begins to further lose it. His vision becomes a little blurrier, his thinking continues to get a little slower, he starts to hear faint sounds, a sound as if you are in a busy restaurant and so many people are talking, and you can't make out a word of what anyone is saying.

He is used to consuming high amounts of hard liquor, and while Jason didn't care about his life like he once did due to the circumstances. He had a sudden urge to ease up to see if just maybe something would change. It was an unusual spur of the moment thing for him that morning. Jason decided instead of drinking 35-40 shots throughout the day, he would drop it down to at most 3 shots that day. Waiting until the withdrawals got absolutely bad enough that he felt the need to drink.

So Jason did just that in the hopes he would clear his mind. It was the auditory hallucinations that pushed him over. Jason went from consuming high amounts of alcohol to no more than 3 shots that day. His body, being so used to high amounts of alcohol, started to freak out. The amount Jason was drinking when things got bad enough, did not feel **enough** to

Jason. Throughout the day, Jason would go from crying, to shaking so badly, to vomiting, to banging his fists against the wall not knowing what the hell to do, to laying down, watching videos, and writing.

"March 12th 6:07 PM, my mind is everywhere... i want hope, i have none. I am trying to fix this, but I don't why, i spent 20 minutes or so crying while looking at a lamp, i just want to die already, but i want to live. There has to be more than this. I'm so miserable, but I don't want to live without alcohol, its the one thing that helps me through everything. What started out as enjoyable, now brings me pain. It's twisted and now... its too late, but maybe not."

Things were building up, and Jason just couldn't figure what all was going on. **Out of his mind, lost and alone, unsure of what to do.** He just got up and drank half a bottle of vodka, and sat on the edge of his bed, and cried. Light turned to darkness, and time passed as Jason was in a state where he felt asleep, but was also awake. It was a very unusual sensation. The clock would strike 4 in the morning on the day of...

# 6. MARCH 13-14TH

"For this is the end of the road. What was light in the eyes of someone with hope, became lifeless of someone who got lost and broken."

Jasons body lie in a state of unusual consciousness, silence surrounds the entire apartment. The outside air being cold and unwelcoming. The state of things is unusually calm. But its not over yet.

Jolted awake, Jason jumps out of bed in a massive panic, and proceeded to run from one room to the next, sweating, out of breath and heart racing. Nothing can calm him down. Jason proceeded to sit on the couch for 10 seconds, then runs to the bathroom, and then back to the couch. Voices are running through his head, with flashing lights drowning out his vision, so much confusion, and so much desperation, he searches for his alcohol. Finding the half full bottle from the night before he drinks half of it and starts to gag. Out of breath still, and confused,

Jason waits out the voices, and the flashing lights, hoping things improve.

**What felt like hours was really only 25 minutes** before things started to improve. This was getting worse, and he knew this. Jason felt like his time was coming, he started to think about his family. What he loved about them, what he hated about them. Every emotion started to flow through him when he thought about his family. He realized they were trying to be there for him before he cut off communication mostly.

The anger he felt, was really quite simple. Jason didn't want to quit alcohol, and he felt his family would try to take that away from him. What a messed up a feeling isn't it? But for someone so desperate for a substance, its understandable. Jason had to make the hardest decision he had ever had to make. Continue on and most likely die. Or seek help and fight like hell to get his life back, whatever that may be.

The light would overtake the darkness in the sky, and the morning would go on. Jason would ponder the idea of seeking help, and what he wanted to do. He decided to lay down, and he thought of everyone he ever loved. While starting to cry, and think of everything that has happened, he shaking lay grabs his phone. He decides to call his mother and father, not to ask for help necessarily, but to just

tell them what's really been going on. His
father was on vacation with his 2nd
mother in china, while his mother was
back in California working.

His father, being in a different time
zone, was in bed when Jason called. And
Jason talked to him, and came clean about
everything. Shocked, and half asleep, the
tone change of his father shook Jason.
Calling his mother after his father, and her
picking up the phone sounding happy,
and then upon hearing Jasons shaky voice,
her tone changed. **The power of a phone
call and the fact that a phone call can
change everything is astounding.** It
wasn't too soon after these calls, that
Jasons father had a family friend pick him

up and take him to the hospital. Which he wanted after talking to his parents. Jason takes one last shot, gets dressed, and as he gets notified that the friend is there, and is waiting in the parking lot. Jason stops to look in the mirror, and what he saw back was very red eyes and a shocked look.

Jason walks out of his apartment, and looks behind at everything while he walks out the door. His life, that apartment, and the pain were all going behind him. He closes the door, and locks it one last time. His legs start shaking horribly, and his heart starts racing as he goes down the staircase. The staircase he dreaded. The outside air blasts him, and his eyes, still filled with tears, start to burn.

He gets into the backseat of the car, and is driven to the hospital. The drive seemed to take forever, though it really didn't. Feeling like an empty shell, weak and damaged, he looks out the window at everything going on in the world around him. It's dreary and dull outside. The world looks depressing and the cold air adds to that mood. The outside world that day truly matched how Jason was feeling on the inside.

Approaching the loading zone to the Emergency Room, the family friend wished Jason the best of luck. Getting out and walking into the entrance of a somewhat busy E.R, he proceeded to the check in desk. Jason gets asked what is going on. Jason tells the woman everything he could.

That he has a bad problem with alcohol, and that his health is bad, and that he suffers from alcohol withdrawals and needs help. The process of questioning was quick, and in a somewhat busy E.R Jason shockingly got taken back in less than 10 minutes. In a quick fashion, they started helping him, and tests were being done.

Once Jasons labs came back, the medical professionals looked shocked, and had made the decision to transfer him to the ICU(Intensive Care Unit). In the meantime the E.R Professionals were administering treatment to help Jason.

Everything was out of whack for him. Looking at the bright lights on the ceiling, and the sounds of people talking, and walking by. Mixing that with the beeping and chimes the machines would make, everything felt like a blur.

**Jason was alone, and couldn't even begin to process all that was going on.** He was questioning whether or not he should have gotten help, or even made those phone calls. Jason didn't know if he was going to be okay. The ICU was busy, and it took a while for Jason to be transferred over which is understandable. He was shocked that he got admitted so quickly. Turns out things were worse than he had thought.

The beeps and chimes become overwhelming but Jason feels comfort in a weird sort of way. Maybe it was the medication to help with he withdrawals, or maybe that even if Jason may have had regrets about asking for help, he felt relieved to hear his parents voices and that he was getting help, even if they weren't there with him. This provided an unusual sense of calmness, despite the crazy around him.

A transporter, and the nurse came to take Jason up to the ICU, and by this time it is dark outside. It had been almost all day, but it all felt so quick. This ride was significant, and it felt like they were going so fast, the lights on the ceiling were blurring almost it seemed. Things felt calm and different. It took a little bit, but they approach the ICU and its dark, except for one room with its door open. Almost like the light at the end of a dark tunnel. Inside of it were 6 different medical professionals circling a bed. They proceeded to move Jason who isn't able to move at all, to the ICU bed from the bed he was transferred over on.

They immediately start hooking Jason up to machines, and start checking everything on him. The bright lights seemed to dim a little bit, tears start to fill in his eyes a bit, as he looks straight up. Wondering in his head just how he got to this point. Time seemed to move slowly, and things started to get dimmer. The dull, dark cloudy day that matched his feelings, started to be forgotten. Jason thought of his family, and the things in his life, from the good moments and the bad ones.

A sense of calm came over him. Things got dimmer, and his eyes started to get more teared up. He felt regret, and he could heard his mother and fathers voices in his head. "I'm sorry, I am so sorry, how did i get this far gone." Thought jason. In an empty ICU room, Jason felt even more calm. The once lit up room that he was brought into, got dark, and the empty shell of someone filled with hope whisked away fast. Jason went into cardiac arrest.

After an effort by the medical team, He wasn't able to be revived. Jason was pronounced dead at 12:09 on the morning of march 14th 2017. All while his family was attempting to travel to him. They never made it in time to say goodbye. Jason lost his life. 27 years, and the life of someone turned upside down, has now come to an end. Jason became another death statistic. Destruction By Alcoholism.

# THE AUTHOR

*I am including the "About The Author" into this book. Mostly to finish off this story. However the book goes on.*

My name is Ian A. McCown, and i am an alcoholic. And i am the person in this story. **I am Jason**, and these events actually did occur. Only i was 21, and the death didn't happen in the real life version of this story. I hope to live a long life. This story, it means the world to me. Just writing it was a big struggle for me.

However, even if it was a struggle, i feel it was the most important thing i could do as a writer. To tell my story. At least part of it! Why did i kill myself off in my own story? To make a point. To show how destructive alcoholism is. I killed myself off in my own story to show you how easily things could have gone in the wrong direction. **I don't want people suffering from this to become a death statistic.**

Some people don't seem to understand addiction, or they do to a point. Some probably know someone who has had, or is currently struggling with addiction to alcohol. This book is to show how devastating alcohol addiction can be, and to help people better understand how messed up ones mind can be because of it.

I got help, i developed a better relationship to my family, and i made a new life for myself. I am so far staying sober, and i hope to keep it that way. This book is in no way a happy book, but way to tell my story.

**The end of "Destruction By Alcoholism". Thank you! Continue on!**

# IVE RELAPSED A FEW TIMES

I have relapsed on a few occasions post my big change in 2017, I want to explain why I relapsed, and what I did about it. I'm adding this chapter in because tonight, I nearly relapsed. And to get those feelings, in my opinion, is okay, just as long you don't act on them! Let's start out with my first one.

In the Beginning of 2018, prior to my first year anniversary of my sobriety, I was a mess. I was struggling with my job at the time. I was working 6 days a week. My commute was two hours round trip, and I only had about 2 hours after work to do anything. Overworked, and miserable is basically what you can coin that up to. Anyways, I began questioning my sobriety, which is common as far as I've seen, and experienced! The pain of my hospital stay was fading away, and all the bad times that motivated me to keep staying sober started fading away as well. I could really only remember the good times. **Pain has a short memory.**

So I bought a little thing of vodka on the way home. After I got home, I ended up drinking it. There wasn't anything dramatic about it, such as what you might see in movies, or television. If you'd see me drinking it, you wouldn't have even guessed I was relapsing.

However, it was a mistake. I felt so much guilt. All this effort I put into my sobriety was damaged that night. The guilt was from failure that I felt, and also from letting down those around me that pushed for me to stay strong with my sobriety. However, I didn't just give up because of the relapse. I had a slip up, which can happen to some, however I got right back into my sobriety after that.

I knew I was better off without alcohol. I knew that I couldn't drink like a normal person. I knew that I was a drinker who drank to ease the problems, often mentally, that I was dealing with. My first sponsor that I ever had, had relapsed, and had been hospitalized multiple times due to alcohol problems. Strongest individual I've ever met with sobriety. So while avoiding relapse is obviously important for many reasons. I didn't blame myself for slipping up, because I am human, and sobriety can be difficult! And when I would see someone relapse, I was always very proud of the person for continuing to try to be sober, even after a slip up, or even multiple slip ups. I mentioned my old sponsor because it gave me hope that, even if I had relapsed, he had relapsed before as well, and continue to stay strong! Which meant I could too.

I always thought I would relapse over something extremely significant happening in my life, however, all of the relapses that I have had were due to problems that weren't even big, and when I did have a significant thing happen in my life, I haven't so far struggled to stay sober through it. It's weird that it's the little things that put me at the most risk.

Tonight, for example, I had a smell of peach vodka in a shot glass. And I had a sudden strong urge to drink it. I really almost did. Luckily I didn't. I wasn't having a bad day, and nothing up to that point was a problem. It just came out of nowhere when I had that smell. Which gave me inspiration to add this chapter In!

Sobriety is... tricky. Make no mistake about it. However, people have relapsed before, like myself! I got right back on the sobriety wagon each time so far. It's also so crazy how you never truly know what may make you want to take a drink. I've identified triggers, however I had thought I had gotten to the point where smelling alcohol wasn't a problem. It really wasn't a problem, but tonight, it was. Which can happen. What matters is that I remember why I do this, and why life is better without alcohol. I can't throw away what

I've worked hard for, and if I do, I'm going to get right back on the sobriety wagon if I can.

# THE PEOPLE I ONCE
# ASSOCIATED WITH

This one is extremely difficult to write, as it brings back memories of people I enjoyed spending time with, but had to stop talking to, for the sake of my own happiness, and sobriety.

I am willing to bet money, that you the reader, have a friend that is an enabler. Imagine you are wanting a relaxing night, and one of your friends drags you out, and hours later, you are wasted, and depressed! It's partially your fault for agreeing to go out, but you would be having a relaxing night most likely, had you not agreed to go out.

What about a significant other? Doesn't have to be a boyfriend, or girlfriend. Could be someone you are dating. I have heard countless stories from people who's significant others were the main cause of their drinking, either by encouragement, or depression from being with them. I myself didn't really go through it, except for breakups, where i would drink excessively. Plain, and simple, you might consider breaking it off with that significant other, friend, family member etc. Which is more easier said then done, but let me say this. You are human, you are trying to thrive in life, you've had it difficult already most likely, and the last thing you need is someone who is becoming part of your possible downfall. So breaking it off with that person might be something to consider. This advice, like my other advice, is mainly for those who have a problem with alcohol.

And make no mistake, It is difficult for me to write, and it is also difficult to even bring up the subject.

Some examples:

1. I knew a girl In Alcoholics Anonymous, who like her mother, was

an alcoholic. However, the girl was trying to get better, and stay sober. Her mother however was not making that same effort. The girl decided to stop talking to her mother, in order to not be tempted, or be in an environment in which she was at risk for relapse. **I agree with what the girl did.**

2. I knew a girl in outpatient rehab who broke up with her boyfriend, due to the fact that he was an enabler, and when sobriety was talked about, he would just deny she had any problems. She knew she had problems, and he wasn't willing to change. She had struggled with alcohol

problems for years, and in and out of facilities. **I agree with her.**

Now those are two examples. I said the two hardest examples. Cutting all contact with a significant other, or a family member. Friends can be hard to stop talking to, however in comparison with a significant other, it generally is easier. Nevertheless, it's disappointing that it can come to that. But understand that I don't think it is selfish to care about ones sobriety, and health. You need to make sure your health, mental health etc. are okay! It's not selfish to want that! And to those who refuse to be there, and supportive of ones sobriety, then I suggest you try to see differently, because shame on you. Nothing bothers me more, then when someone is trying to get help, and improve their life because they have a problem, and someone is just downplaying it, or being an enabler. Need I say more? Am I being too harsh? Perhaps. But at the same time, too many people die from alcoholism, so many people are struggling trying to get help, and there aren't enough people in the world willing to be there for someone struggling.

**End Of Chapter**

(The next two chapters are interactive! It's for those struggling with alcohol. Feel free to read through or skip!)

# YOU'VE BEEN HERE BEFORE?

You've been here before haven't you? Maybe you've questioned if you have a problem for example, or maybe you are just a curious mind looking for more information! Well, I am glad you are here! Alcohol problems unfortunately plague a lot of people. Too many people for that matter, and if I can do my part to help someone, then I am happy with that. This is a book of relation, and a little bit of guidance when I can give it. I want you to mething, if you are someone struggling with alcohol at least, and it's a rather simple thing.

1. Get a piece of paper, along with a pen/pencil.

2. Title it "Alcohol Is bad for me because:".

3. Write down why alcohol is bad for you.

4. Now, after writing that, write down "Why I am strong:".

5. Now write why you are strong.

Now hold on to it, and let it be a reminder as to where you are now, and look at it as much as you need too. I know, it's a little bit of work, but seeing it written down can be beneficial I think. Now next question! How much did you lie on the writing? Don't worry, I understand it! But you probably held back a little on writing it, or left out details! It's okay if you did! I've done the same thing, but remember what I am saying however. If you aren't honest with, and about yourself, it might just hold you back further!

This is all a process, and it's not easy to think about how alcohol is impacting your life! Just the thought of giving up alcohol can be a challenge, and I understand how you feel about giving it up. I've been there before… each person has to put in a different amount of effort, depending on the individual. Some people will be able to easily make changes, others? Not so much. But I need to warn you of something. Some people don't end up changing until something catastrophic happens. Don't get to that point. Again, don't get to that point.

You do not want to end up being forced to quit alcohol under a circumstance such as this! **For example, if you drive drunk, and end up killing someone. And you get thrown in jail, and are now forced to stop drinking, as well as your life changing forever because of your reckless actions.**

Anyone who has ever driven drunk, and hoped so much that they could make it home safely, and not getting pulled over, or in an accident in the process, knows this fear all too well! And I don't want to see you, the reader, or anyone else for that matter, throwing everything away. It's not worth it. Do not get this point. You have loved ones, friends, and a life with potential. If you are suffering from alcohol problems at the moment of reading these very words, I am willing to bet you aren't entirely aware of what you are doing in life. You may just be extremely oblivious to the decisions you are making! Think about yourself in the past where you didn't have a problem with alcohol, and then think about what that past version of you would think of the current version of you. Would they think you are making the correct decisions? It's an interesting question... and a question I cannot answer for you.

# I'M LOST AT SEA

It's something odd to say. "I am lost at sea". What does it mean for you? Well let's look at it like this.

1. **You don't know where you are.**

2. **You don't know whether or not you will be okay.**

3. **You can't see where land and life is.**

4. You feel as if one mistake could cost you everything.

5. How long will you survive while lost at sea.

Let's try a different thing. You are lost on a windy mountain road, and it's so foggy, that you can't see anything around you.

1. You can't see ahead of you, or around you.

2. One mistake could mean you end up driving off a cliff.

3. You are lost.

4. You feel uneasy about the situation.

5. You don't know if you will get through this drive.

Much like problems with alcohol, those two situations can be relevant to you... maybe. Much like like alcoholism, you may feel lost, alone, maybe on edge, or unsure how long you will go on with the current state of things. Maybe you feel as if one decision can destroy everything.

This isn't a good feeling, and a feeling that I know all too well. It should help to give you perspective. I want to help you see what you might not have seen before.

Do you feel you can relate to those examples I gave? If so, it means you are one step closer to understanding yourself a little more! I hope.

So let's get a little more "Self Help" here now.

1. Get out that piece of paper I had you write on.

2. Now get your pen/pencil.

3. Write out which example you feel you can relate to more. Then write out why.

4. After that, I want you to write "Drinking Triggers:".

5.  Then write out things that trigger you to drink. And please... be honest about it.

Now that you have written out your triggers, I want you to look at the paper again. Read it to yourself... and after reading it, I want you to once again hold on to it. We're not done yet. The next time you will need is in in the "Motivation" chapter!

# YOU CAN LIVE A LIFE WITHOUT ALCOHOL!

(Assuming you have safely withdrawn from alcohol, and are starting the process of living life sober) Sobriety can be a very tricky, and difficult thing. However, in my experience, I'm better off being sober. I am happier, I feel healthier(to an extent! I say this because I need to gain more weight), my ability to cope is a lot better!

Which I'm shocked by, mostly because I would often drink to cope with things, so I thought I would have much more difficulty coping without it. Turns out I cope better without it! Mostly because I learned that with alcohol, I was masking my problems, and without it, I tend to face them more, thus leading to a solution.

I am able to think more clearly as well! Which took a bit. For the first year or so, I felt like I was in a fog, and it was something that I disliked. However, when I got out of that fog, I felt much more stable, and rational in comparison.

Odds are high I think, that if you are fully in addict mode with alcohol, then you probably think you would have extreme difficulty being sober! However, there are options out there such as inpatient rehab, outpatient rehab, Alcoholics Anonymous, therapy etc. to help you deal with these things! Other people have thought this way! I have thought this way, but I was wrong.

I won't bullshit you though! I've read things where people kind of sugarcoat sobriety. That's always annoyed me. So let me say this. It can be challenging, and testing. You may get strong cravings, and you may have times where you are struggling with staying sober. Staying strong, and seeking help is important. I don't want to sugarcoat things for you. Hell, I even killed myself off in my own story "Destruction By Alcoholism" to prove a point of how destructive alcoholism can be! So I hope you know I'm trying to be as honest as I can with you!

So I will end this short chapter saying this! Sobriety can be challenging, but I have found that it is worth it, and I am much happier being sober, in comparison to destroying myself with alcohol. Addiction has taken so many lives, and i wish to see those statistics lowered to zero. While I know that most likely would never happen, if they can be reduced... then that is

# I WANT TO BE YOUR FIRST SUPPORTER

Time for me to give you a pep talk. When I was on the verge of losing it all. I didn't have any sort of literature that I could relate too. I didn't really have any sort of person cheering me on until after I got help either. Let me be that to you, the reader, who may be going through so much stuff.

If your life is being controlled by substance, I understand it. That was me as well. If you feel you can't quit, because

you've tried it before with no success, well,
I've been there as well. If you look into the
mirror and are disgusted by what is
looking back at you, well, I've been there
more times to even count. The reason I am
writing this, is for you! It's not for fame, or
money, it's to help. I write what I write for
you. So I want you to know from the
bottom of my heart, that even if we have
different lives, we relate in a few ways I am
sure. Which means that I know you are
capable of seeking help! It's of course
obvious that withdrawing safely from
alcohol is important. Had I not been
hospitalized for my withdrawals, I would
have been in even more danger. So safety

is of course important. I am rooting for you to be safe, and to safely get off alcohol.

Second of all, I am rooting for you with your sobriety! You will be entering into a new world when it comes to sobriety! Luckily there are people who are willing to help make things easier, and more clear in the sobriety process. Rehabilitation centers, Alcoholics Anonymous, and therapy, among other things are great places to start. We get the pain of sobriety, and we get struggles that come day to day. We understand it, and we hear you. I hear you.

Third, and finally. I am rooting for you to become a better human being as well. It was no secret that prior to getting help, I was a mess, and had so many problems. However upon getting help, I started to make changes! Which had a positive impact, and helped me to become a better person overall. I am rooting for you to do the same! We all have flaws, and struggles, but one thing our world lacks is kindness. Things just can be too dark, so if I shed a little light into the darkness of your life, let's hope you can shed light into another's.

None of this is easy, but I am rooting for you! I am rooting for your happiness, I am rooting for your sobriety, and I am rooting for your kindness. My name is Ian, what's yours? Write below.

# TRAUMA

Trauma... be it from a young age, or something more recent, can throw people off the edge into a situation that they have never been in before. Trauma can also be a major blow to someone already going through addiction. Perhaps losing a loved one in a car accident at a young age, and the pain catches up to you, or maybe a series of breakups that pushes you to the breaking point. Trauma is there, and it comes in many forms.

Are you someone who drinks to help manage depression? Maybe life is throwing so much at you at once, and for so long now it seems, that substance is your go-to when it comes to dealing with it? Or maybe you lost a significant other, and you feel as if you just cannot stay sober, because all you think about sober is your loss? You ask yourself how you can possibly live your life without substance, or you just can't even fathom going through recover, ALONG with everything else going on! These are extremely difficult examples, and frankly there aren't any easy answers, but I can maybe offer some advice, and hope.

First, and foremost, I have seen people who have been through traumatic experiences get help, and become okay after effort. My god, some of the stories I have heard shook me to my core. But I learned something from the things I have heard. People can show the most strength during the worst times. Even in the darkest of times, people have found the light. I find that relying on those around you, can be beneficial. Especially if you know someone who has also struggled with substance. Take me for example. The first person I related to the most wasn't even an alcoholic, but in fact a heroin addict. It's crazy to think about, but it's true. Remember, that you have strength, you have the chance to have a life, and you must not throw it all away. I want you the reader to be okay, and I want you to be able to live happily!

I can't even imagine what you are probably feeling if you are someone who has been through a lot of trauma. But I want you to be happy, and I want you to get better. I am rooting for you to get better. Here's what I've learned from other people on how they've dealt with things. It's not a one size fits all type thing. But maybe you might find something useful.

1. Motivation can be make or break. Your reasons to want to pull through difficult situations are important in my opinion. If you want my opinion on this, what would happen if you your family members lost you due to alcohol abuse, or if your kids are left with one parent, or without a parent because they lost you to alcohol abuse! What would go through their minds if someone they have memories with, becomes a memory to them. Think about it.

2. How you get help is important. Alcohol withdrawals can be dangerous. Enough said there. You

must take the proper steps when
becoming sober.

3.  Immediately surrounding yourself
with people who are like you can be
beneficial. The immediate advice that
you may get, could prove useful for
the next day, and so on. Places like
A.A, or Rehab Centers can be the
place the best options.

4.  I know you have probably tried to
get help before, but you've fallen
behind, or you might think alcohol is
the only way you can be happy.
Others have felt this way, and have
managed to pull through it. It doesn't

always happen on the first try I've found. Not even for me.

# MY ROUGH TIME

I thought for a moment I could write about the drinking urges I have now, and why. Perhaps to just write it down for myself to look back on, or for you to read, and perhaps relate to. If you wish to skip this chapter, I completely understand.

It is July 15, 2021. And for a while I felt something getting worse with me in regards to my mental health. I didn't know what, just felt more on edge, and anxious for no reason. Anxiety for no reason is common with me, however this felt different. Much more like a fearful, irrational anxiety. I can say that these feelings started out towards the end of June while on a trip to visit family. Towards the end of the trip, I was stuck in a hotel room, and had a sleeping schedule that was absolutely garbage, among other things. I could feel a slight sense of detachment from reality, only when my anxiety was especially bad.

To explain further, I suffer from Derealization. Which is where you basically feel detached from things. Everything looks alien to me, things are off. It's been a problem since I was 14 years old. Generally in the past, The sensation would be persistent for quite a while, and then go away. Something like a severe panic attack would spawn these feelings for me, and then they would linger. The feeling of detachment would generally occur during the panic attack.

Anyways it stopped around 18 years old, and for years i didn't have any issues. Until a few days ago, when one morning I had a severe panic attack. One in which I felt these feelings, and these feelings freaked me out to the point that I wanted to call 911. Luckily I did not. But since that occurred, I am now dealing with these lingering feelings. And the problem is how I deal with it. Because it has been so long since dealing with it, that I have forgotten how to deal with it. In the past I managed it well, but now? I'm struggling like no other. In the past it was one of the reasons I started drinking excessively, and of course I cannot do that. However the urge to drink has been quite strong since then, but I'm staying strong. As difficult as it is.

It's truly amazing how something out of nowhere can knock you down so quickly, and absolutely destroy your ability to deal with anxiety. I also want to point out that I have seen multiple psychologists, and psychiatrists over the past decade, and schizophrenia wasn't anything that was considered when diagnosing me with my problems. This is just something I yet again have to deal with, and I will try to push through these problems!

I'm writing this book to help others, and I feel the need to write what I'm writing. Mostly due to the fact that I've read some self help books, and sometimes the author of the book makes it seem like their life is so perfect, and without issue. I'm not bashing or anything, but I feel it is important to show you that I am not like that! We are all human, and wow do things come out of nowhere to knock us down sometimes. That is only human, and we just have to stay strong through our problems! I can only hope that what you've read so far has help in a way!

# RELIANCE UPON LOVED ONES

"Hello, my name is Ian, and I am not a family person!" -Not a family person Ian.

So, I'm not really a family person, which means a few different things for me.

1.  I never attend family gatherings.

2.  I don't respond to calls, or messages as much as I should.

3.  Im generally in my head, and on my own a lot!

Generally that's me! My family knows this about me, and that's how it is. However, I have found that being around family, and talking to them, is extremely beneficial to my mental health, and sobriety! Which is why I have made the effort to be more "family" like.

This doesn't apply to just family, it can be friends, or significant others as well! It's extremely nice knowing that I can call someone, regardless of the hour, and talk to them if I need to! The same goes for them. And i feel it is important to say that loneliness was one of the hardest parts in the beginning stages of my sobriety. I feel as if it almost keeps you in line when family members are keeping an eye on you. Because if I had gotten out of the hospital, and spent all my time alone, I would have relapsed so fast! Talking to family, and staying with them even, was extremely helpful when I was struggling with anxiety, cravings, and all the fun stuff with sobriety.

So I feel it important to say, that if you have family members for example, then you should consider seeing if you can rely on them in your time of struggle. It's something that can help alot, and I've seen my fair share of people NOT want to rely on anyone else. This was mainly due to people not wanting to ask for help! Mainly because they don't want to come off as weak. Which I understand somewhat, however, sobriety is no laughing matter, and aside from my advice on therapy for example, family members can be a big help! As long as they are wanting to help.

# LET'S TALK MOTIVATION

Let's talk about motivation shall we? Motivation in general, is important in life. The motivation to succeed with your career, or the motivation to make improvements! Those are examples, but what about sobriety? What's your motivation? It's a simple question, but I guarantee you have a complex answer. You may say "I want to feel healthier", or "I don't want to feel trapped by a substance". Which are things people have said of course, but think about it more than that!

You want to feel healthier? Okay, people have said that before, but elaborate! How do you want to feel healthier, and what are you going to do to achieve that goal? It may sound confusing, if so I apologize, but I believe that if you are motivated to make a change, you need to understand your motivations as much as you can. In my opinion, I think a stronger motivation to change, can be more successful, than being less motivated.

Something else I feel the need to talk about it, is the why. If I was forced to make changes in my life, I can safely say that I would have failed early on in sobriety. What I feel was successful for me, was the fact that I was the one who decided to get help. It was all on my own. So think about it like this. If someone is forced to get help for alcohol problems, and they weren't the ones who decided to make that change, how successful will they be? Just because you think they have a problem, doesn't mean they think that way! If I was forced into changing, not by my own choice, I wouldn't have the motivation to change, because I don't fully believe I have a problem. In turn I would most likely fail! Does that make sense?

I want you to understand your problems more, and I could never consider you an alcoholic, that's not my decision, I believe. Other people have considered me an alcoholic, but I never believed it, or felt motivated to change, until I considered myself an alcoholic. Of course, I should have listened to others, because they were correct. However, I didn't want to change until I realized things. And I'm not saying to ignore those who suggest you may be an alcoholic, or want you to get help. I just want you to also realize your problems, and really think about them! Otherwise, I dont feel like things can change. Understanding the problem, helps find the solution!

I was motivated by a few different things. And I will list them! Why don't you get your piece of paper ready.

**1. I was getting weaker, and weaker.**

**My health was going downhill, and in**

hindsight, had I not gotten help, i would have been dead within a month.

2. My family was worried about me. I was distancing myself from them, and It was starting to get to me.

3. My life was going downhill in general. I didn't have a job, and I didn't want to do anything else. I was trapped by a substance, and I wanted out.

4. My withdrawals were destroying me.

5. My depression was getting worse. Had I not made changes, and had my

**depression gotten worse, I probably would have become suicidal.**

Those are my motivations. I'm honest with you, so be honest with yourself. Write down your motivations.

# THE PAPER I HAD YOU WRITE ON

This book... is your book. I write for you, and I want to help you. I wanted to do my part to help those who are in the shoes that I was once in. I didn't have this. I couldn't relate to other self help things that I read. It was all such a confusing time for me. Frankly sobriety is a tricky thing to do. But I have faith in you. Whether or not you are wanting to change your life, or you are already sober. And if you are just a curious mind, well I'm glad you took the chance to read this. I hope I wrote a book that you could understand, and one that you feel you learned something from. Take that piece of paper, and look at it. What do you see? What information is on there? And do you see your problems, and motivations? Now hold onto it, and remember it. Are you ready to start a new chapter in your life?

# BE A GOOD PERSON

We live in a world that, if you look back 10 years ago, people aren't there for each other as much. You can blame it on a number of things, such as politics, social media, and changes in overall society. I hate that things are like this. Not to mention that being there for people with a substance abuse problem is absolutely key. Unfortunately, when you have less people who are there for each other, it takes away much needed help. So I feel I need to say this. If you differ politically, or your other views differ, for example, you shouldn't just automatically stop being there for someone who may need it. And I get it, people can be asshats when it comes to views, but why all the people cutting each other out of their lives?

Regardless, this is how society is nowadays it seems. While you may not do it, some others do that. And I don't care where your views, or politics are. What I care about is different. I want more people to be there for each other! In general, and also if someone you care for is struggling, and needs a person to talk to. Besides, I've always found that talking to other alcoholics is helpful with sobriety! And I have seen differing views in meetings start arguments. So you, yeah you reading this, you might attend some type of group, or meeting, and you might have someone differ from you. I don't want that to stop you from talking to them. Unless things are extreme! So just try to be there, and keep the politics, and differing views for example, out of the conversation.

# THE AUTHOR

Ian A. McCown.

This is Sobriety & Strength. A book of help, honesty, and overall general information. I've written to the best of my ability to help those who may need it. When I needed help, I didn't have this type of book. Yes, there are other self help books about alcoholism, but none I could relate to! So after learning more about sobriety, both with research, and my own experiences, I decided to write what I wish I could of had back then. Thank you for

reading this, and i hope it is everything
that you were looking for. Thank you.

Printed in Great Britain
by Amazon